Awakening the Vulnerable Heart

Awakening
THE VULNERABLE HEART

Catherine Thomas

All rights reserved. No part of this publication may be reproduced, distributed, or transmitted in any form by any means, including photocopying, recording, or other electronic methods without the prior written permission of the author, except in the case of brief quotations embodied in reviews and certain other noncommercial uses permitted by copyright law. For permission requests, write to the author at the address below.

Copyright © 2023 Catherine Thomas

Photographs by Catherine Thomas

Published by Catherine Thomas
Cedarburg, Wisconsin 53012

catherine.thomas.wi@gmail.com

ISBN 979-8-218-20218-7

Library of Congress Control Number: 2023908335

Designed by Tell Tell Poetry

Printed in the United States of America

First Printing, 2023

To three women who supported my odyssey:

MW, who met me at the trailhead

SC, who guided me off the crumbling bluff

and

BWK, who kept me beautifully grounded throughout.

Contents

Soft Shell	2
Fool's Gold	4
Saving Grace	6
Haunted	7
High Dive	9
Freehand	10
Rebuilding	11
Bravest Act	12
Navigating Reality	14
Crossroads	15
Hiding in Plain Sight	16
Resurgence of Reassurance	17
Foyer	18
Asked and Answered	20
Evermore	22
Scourge Survival	23
Lucid Daydream	24
Certain Certainty	25
Wasteland	27
Blinders	29
Present of Presence	30
Leap of Faith	31
Lighthouse and Ship	32
Kismet	34
Longing	35
Floating Dock	36

Angel	38
Sweetest Slumber	39
Rejuvenescence	40
Heart of the Matter	41
As-Is	42
Unutterable	43
Pronouncement	44
Beautiful Torture	45
Outside of the Box	46
Clear Vision	47
Autumnal Desire	48
Musing for My Muse	49
Roseate Heart	50
Agony and Rapture	51
Paint a Picture	52
Succumb	53
Famine	55
Moth and Flame	56
Reticence	58
One	59
Awake and Alive	61
Resolution	62
Weight of Risk	63
Revelation	64
Force of Attraction	65
Crossing Over	66
Duality	68
Death of Muse	69

Push and Pull	70
Soulless	71
End Credits	72
Anahata	73
Reframing	74
Autumn's Lesson	75
Lofty Thoughts	76
Nature's Nurturing Nudge	78
Lotus Heart	80
Impactful Impact	82
Silent Seduction	84
Here and Now	85
Mercurial	86
Self As Sapling	87
Coming to Equilibrium	88
Resilience	89
Ajna	91
Getaway Train	93
Lost and Found	94
Rebirth	96
About the Author	98

Awakening the Vulnerable Heart

Soft Shell

The tortoise
Overtly carries
Her home on her back
To keep
Others out.
I
Covertly carry
Mine inside of my heart
To draw
Others in.

Fool's Gold

Infinite circles
Conceal realities unspoken
Causing the wearer
To be quelled
By the token.
Whilst heart and spirit
Soar to places anew
Maelstrom
Enfetters the body
To its assigned
Pew.

Saving Grace

As trifling chatter flowed
Heartily as water
From a severed pipe
She positioned her hand
Across her heart
Knowing whose words
Truly
Made her feel
Alright.

Haunted

The home
I used to make
Feels like
A necropolis.
The decision
Hanging in the balance
Torments like
A demon.

High Dive

Jumping off
The high dive
Is daunting.
Moving forward requires
Hitting bottom
And having faith
In resurfacing.
Backing away
Means hovering blindly
Over a safety net of concrete.
Breathe... Focus... Release.

Freehand

The cards
Have been laid
On the table
Deftly revealing
Her hand.
She exhales
In gratitude
For those
Who with her
Stand.

Rebuilding

A life
Stripped down
To studs
Now awaits
Finishing touches.

Bravest Act

Just because
The flesh underneath
Has atrophied
Doesn't make
Yanking off the bandage
Any less painful.

Navigating Reality

My elevator
Is stalled
Between
Blooming enchantment
And
Numbing despair.

Crossroads

As she embarked
On the daily routine
Of removing tarnish
From her sterling mask
Of strength
She pondered
Whether surrender and vulnerability
Better fit her goal
Of attaining
A genuine life.

Hiding in Plain Sight

Veiled behind
Positivity strength and humor
Lies
My vulnerability.

Resurgence of Reassurance

Wrap
Your arms
Around me
Bury
Your face
In my hair
Swear
You'll never
Let go.

Foyer

Her shoes
Occupy a spot
By your door.
My heart's
Being steered
Towards an alluring
Shore.

Asked and Answered

With life
In the balance
The time
Has finally come
To follow
My heart.

Evermore

If days of reckoning
These indeed be
May memories
Of your magnetic soul
Be carried forever
With me.

Scourge Survival

Social distancing
May save my life
But only breathing
In unison with you
Will save
My soul.

Lucid Daydream

What gives me the fortitude
To endure the solitude
Of interminable reclusion
Is the delicious aspiration
Of an absence of latitude
Between me and you.

Certain Certainty

Sweet sentiments
Surviving situational separation and scourge
Set in stone
Steadfastly subsist.

Wasteland

As everyday normalcy
Is viciously uprooted
I remain planted
In humor and love.
Can I count
On you
To buttress
My garden?

Blinders

I close my eyes
To the folly
Of current affairs
Focusing instead
On the affairs
Of my heart.

Present of Presence

I am not
A woman wooed
By flowers or diamonds.
The sweetness of your words
The sound of your voice
And the realization
Of the abolition
Of situational separation
Will suffice.

Leap of Faith

Imagine
If your body and mind
Followed the lead
Of what
Your heart deemed
A sure thing.

Lighthouse and Ship

Although
The wayfaring ship
Makes no physical contact
With the lighthouse
Its magnificent radiance
Nevertheless
Affects the trajectory
Of her journey.

Kismet

Across
Many lifetimes
Our souls
Have exquisitely
Harmonized.

Longing

I long…
I long to embrace you
Holding tight to the physical manifestation
Of the soul
That's touched my heart.
I long to collapse
Into your arms
In a fit of laughter
As you teasingly caress me
Releasing me of my need to always be strong.
I long to break down the walls
Tear down the fences
And dissolve the technicalities.
I long…

Floating Dock

I'm your safe harbor in the vastness of the unbound ocean
There are no lighthouses leading to me
Only sanguine circles.

Moor yourself to my steadfast planks
And together
We will ride out
Exuberant wave… after exuberant wave… after exuberant wave.

Fate makes no promise of next week forever or tomorrow
We are simply entangled with one another
Right here right now.

As you drift back to familiar shores
Gaze into my eyes
Until the expanse between us
Becomes too great.

When you recount the tale
Of how passion and infatuation were stronger
Than fiber chain or wire
May you forever think of me.

Angel

The thought of her words
Being the first
To welcome his spirit
Back into his body
Every morning
And the last
To touch his soul
Each night
Made her eyes sparkle.

Sweetest Slumber

I think about falling asleep
In your embrace
Right arm grazing my hip
Stubbled cheek pillowed in my hair.
The chaos inside and out
Ceasing its fury
Leaving us blissfully
Without a care.

Rejuvenescence

Lay your head
In my lap
Close your eyes
I'll tenderly kiss
The stars back
Into your soul.

Heart of the Matter

Even
If yours
Is broken
It'll always
Be whole
In mine.

As-Is

Messy bun
And
Bare feet
I present myself
To you
My sweet.

Unutterable

If only
You had
A clue
How much
You've made
My heart
Sing.

Pronouncement

The only head
I wish
To turn
Is yours.

Beautiful Torture

He
Unbeknownst
Holds my heart
In a quadrilateral
Of metal and glass.
I
Unabashedly resolute
Wish to hold him
In a ceaseless embrace.

Outside of the Box

I may never
Plant a kiss
On your cheek
But you've left
A permanent mark
On my heart.

Clear Vision

If granted
One wish
It'd be
For you
To see
Me with
Fresh eyes.

Autumnal Desire

As the soft
Fall breezes
Caress my cheek
I longingly wish
It was
You.

Musing for My Muse

How can I not
Stay optimistic
In the midst
Of certain uncertainty
When the same Universe
Brought me
The unexpected joy
Of you.

Roseate Heart

Empirical brain
Delineates reality
To roseate heart.
Her silence bespeaks
Not concession
But recalcitrance.

Agony and Rapture

The momentary pain
Of physical impingement
Is a small price to pay
For the ultimate reward
Of an eternally ecstatic existence
With you.

Paint a Picture

A puerile symbol
Will never
Be a substitute
For the electricity
Of my touch
Or
The heat
Of my breath.

Succumb

Altho
U know
My kryptonite
The notion
Of being driven
Insane
In ur embrace
Puts a smile
On my
Face.

Famine

I had
No idea
The extent
Of my
Hunger
Until I
Partook
Of your
Succulence.

Moth and Flame

I think of us as a two-part epoxy
Our separation of horizonless miles
Preventing an incendiary reaction.
When we finally
Become commingled
Our roughened veneers
Will only facilitate
The process of bonding.

Reticence

I silence
My mouth
From speaking
But my heart
Refuses
To play along.

One

Imagine
Becoming so entwined
The only barrier
Between us
Is the scent of
My lavender perfume.

Awake and Alive

When the portal
Of our bodies
Opens the vortex
Of our souls
I will gaze
Into your eyes.

Resolution

Savor what is
Or risk it all
A knotty decision
Onto my valorous
Heart falls.

Weight of Risk

If
I open
My heart
To you
There is
No going
Back.

Revelation

I was brave
I spoke my heart
We'll see.

Force of Attraction

Two moons
Orbit
The same
Luminous body.
Only time
Will reveal
Which exerts
The strongest pull.

Crossing Over

Grab my hand
And join me
On the other
Side of decision.

Duality

She is your
Soulmate
I am your
Lighthouse.

Death of Muse

Just because
He accompanies
You to the door
And holds it
Wide open
Doesn't guarantee
He'll be following
Right behind you.

Push and Pull

The pain
Of thinking
About losing
What I never had
Breaks my heart.

Soulless

You've chosen
To vanish
During waking hours
And taunt me
With your text tone
In my dreams.

End Credits

You met me
In the trough of despair
Accompanied me
To the threshold of possibilities
Then exited
To the realm of memories.

Anahata

Only time
Will tell
If I'm in
The bargaining stage
Or seeing
Through Anahata.

Reframing

No matter
How beautiful
An image may be
It cannot be contained
In a physical frame
If it's only
A mirage.

Autumn's Lesson

Singular leaves
Initiate the process
Of transformation
Before the entire tree
Is set afire.

Lofty Thoughts

As the sun
Gracefully exits
Perception
One day closer
Is absolute
Restoration.

Nature's Nurturing Nudge

Not unlike
A deciduous tree
The human soul
Eases into a state
Of rejuvenation
After achieving
Glorious transformation.

Lotus Heart

Only
With optimal footing
And conscientious caretaking
Will the floweret
Bloom.

Impactful Impact

Some snowflakes
Travel far
To singularly disappear
Upon impact.
Other snowflakes
Travel far
To collectively combine
Upon impact
Into something larger.

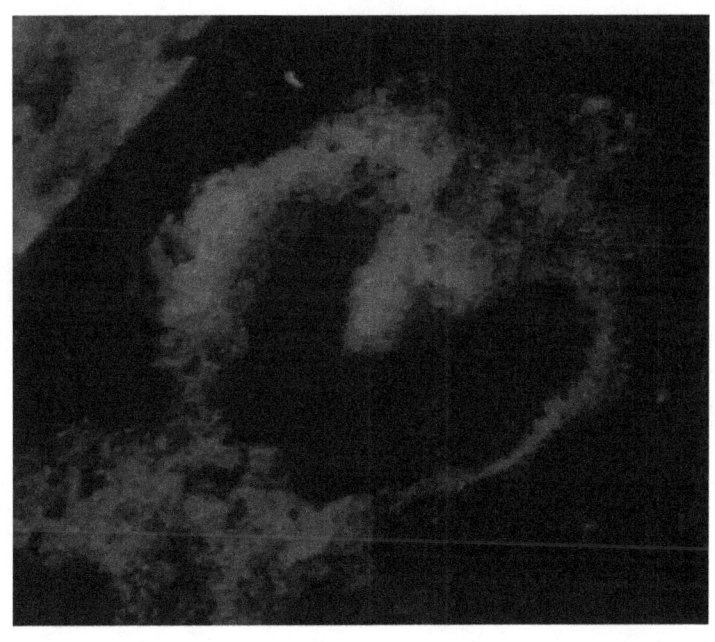

Silent Seduction

Falling snow
Delicately dominates
Terra firma.
I dream
Of being
Cozily ensconced
With you.

Here and Now

In this space of
Contemplation
Devoid of external
Validation
Heart, body, spirit and mind
Become seamlessly
Aligned.

Mercurial

Whilst the bullish wind
Molests her most vulnerable branches
Firmly established fortitude
Holds her ground.

Self As Sapling

I had to break
To get strong.
Now that I'm strong
I refuse to break again.
Ever.

Coming to Equilibrium

Eyes regaining focus
Heart recalibrating
Arms encircling core
Once shallow breaths
Deepening
Embracing hope
Banishing regret.

Resilience

Throughout this journey
I will breathe
I will bend
But
I will refuse
To break.

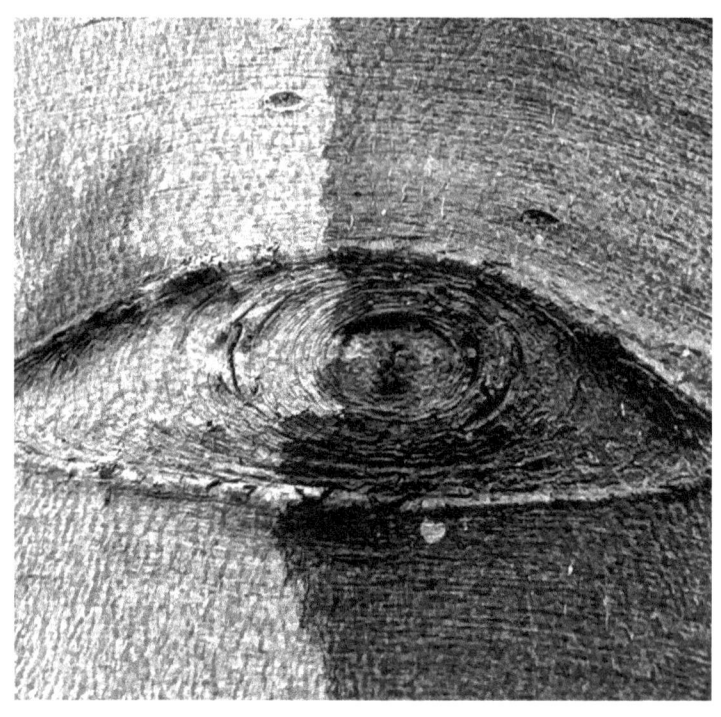

Ajna

Sometimes
A scar
Isn't the disillusionment
Of what was
But the beginning
Of what's
Meant to be.

Getaway Train

I lost myself
In the idea
Of what could be
To survive
What was.

Lost and Found

You were
A beautiful stop
On the
Brave path
To the
Unknown.

Rebirth

For all the
Stress
For all the
Fear
For all the
Uncertainty
I am
Here.

About the Author

Catherine Thomas is passionate about high-octane coffee, forest bathing, and holding space for the stories of those met along the way. *Awakening the Vulnerable Heart* is her first book.

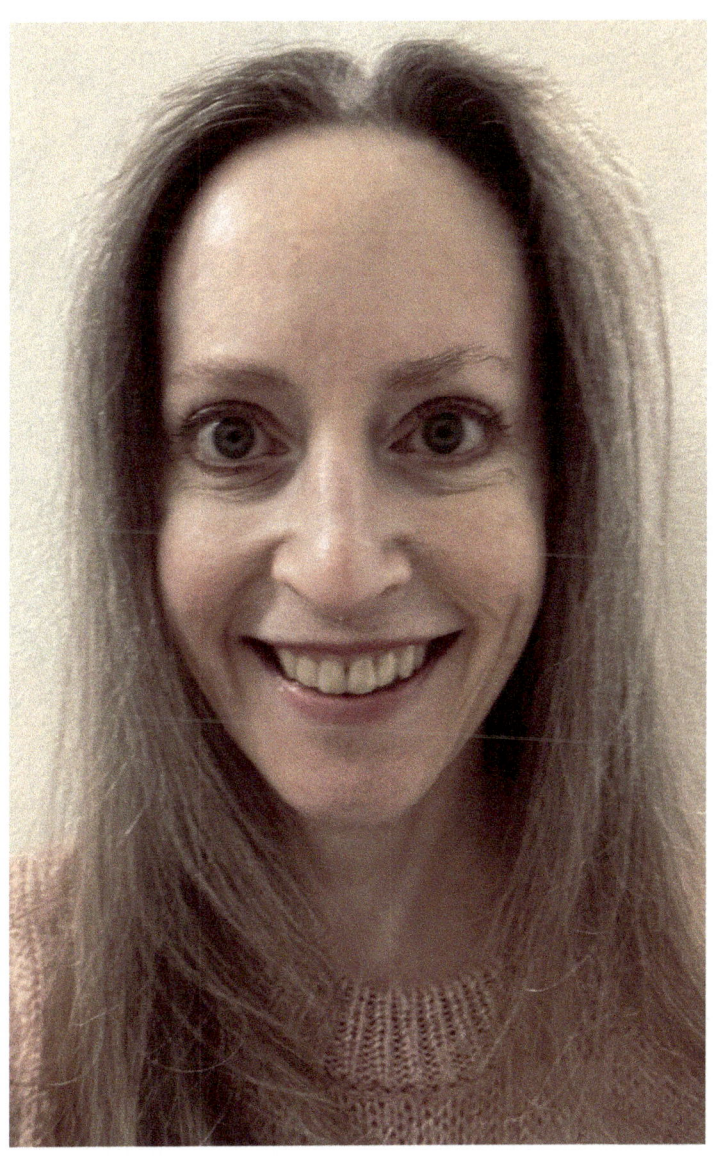

www.ingramcontent.com/pod-product-compliance
Lightning Source LLC
Chambersburg PA
CBHW072201100426
42738CB00011BA/2490